Flood Editions

THREE ROANS IN

THE SHALLOWS, ONE

OF THEM BLUE

Selected Poems

MERRILL GILFILLAN

Published by Flood Editions

www.floodeditions.com

ISBN 979-8-9857874-6-7

Design and composition by Crisis

Printed in Canada on acid-free, recycled paper

Flicker Feathers   1

Song: Forks of the Smoky Hill   2

Solstice Letter   3

Water and Song   7

Spiral Eddy   8

Proposed Elegy for Hart Crane   9

Crayola da Gamba   10

"All Is Well"   11

From the Erstwhile Forks of the Grand   12

Piss Ant and Peony   17

Winterberry   18

The Right to Dance   20

Song   21

Days a Year   22

Ute Note   29

Doll's Eyes   30

July 12, 1990   31

from Penstemon Bearings   32

*

Lines in the Middle of May   37

Allday Purcell   38

Tulip Trees   39

Gentle Rain   42

Night Sky, Pawnee Creek   43

Odoratum   44

Photo Dropping from an Herbal   45

Old Friend on the Quiet Side Far Away   47

Blue Ridge: Streams Are Roaring   48

A Grove on the Musselshell   49

The Music It Was Set To   53

August Evening   54

Morning with Chokecherries   55

Constellation: "Bread Alone"   56

Salute: On Peoples Creek   57

Something for John Clare   59

Roan Mountain: Vireos Sing Falling Water   60

As the Seas Rise   61

From, Their Clouds   62

Meal for an Anasazi Boy   63

Nota Bene   64

The Pencil   65

Ballad Exponential   66

from Four Poems Regarding "The Horses"   69

Ballad Circumstantial   70

Fodderwing   73

Ballad Abstract   74

*

Last Night We Saw and Heard Ms. Fleming   79

So They Say   80

With the Unknown Pawnee Master   81

Damsels 82

To a Man with Cold-hearted Children 84

Falling Folds 85

Li Po Should Know 86

More on the Roan 87

Red Hills 88

Traveler's Tune 90

Undanceable 91

Romanian Elegy 98

Scuppernong 99

Barter: Idle Thoughts of Bodmer 100

Three Settings 101

Constellation: "The Tennessee Waltz" 103

Walking with Cheese 104

Two Hawks 107

Song Near No Heart 108

All Along 109

On a Phrase from the Confucian Odes 110

Bull Run in October 111

*

from Tunes Meant for Whistling 127

Rabbit Mountain 139

A Nap by the Kickapoo 141

from Una Dozzina 142

An Ann Arbor Memory 147

Systole Variations 149

Night Train 151

*

Black Cove: The Nantahalas   155

The Bark of the Dog   156

Hunter's Sky   161

A *Tazza* for Ray   162

An English Poem   164

Dictum   166

The Serpent   167

Constellation: "Fox and Geese"   173

The Road to Hi Hat   174

Paschal Letter   175

Cradle Knoll   178

from The Road to Town   179

Sky in Amber   180

Semper Fi   181

Midnight Coffee   182

Knock On   183

A *Nostos* for Johnny Never Misses   184

Elegy 1024   185

Aker Inkling   186

Salal   187

from Tell Us About the Tang   191

Swannanoa   192

Even Near Saltwater   193

For Jim   194

The Oaks Have Yet to Break   195

Blue Ridge: Blossoms on the Feral Trees   196

High in the Bighorns   197
from Fall (The Seasons)   198

*

Oriole Diary   203
Treehouse *Haibun*   205
Warbler *Haibun*   211

*

NOTES AND ACKNOWLEDGMENTS   217

FLICKER FEATHERS

for a Fall wedding

Woman on the lawn with wine,
pick up summer for a broken book,
rinse your voice in aster
and the lace of Queen Anne,
stall for speechlessness,
kneel in the weeds, soak.

Man in the woods (a whiskey),
stamp, make noise over breakage,
take these five feathers, cornyellow
and horsehair brown, arranged
in a fan shape, finely pointed
and turning in your fingers, home.

SONG: FORKS OF THE SMOKY HILL

Season through place,
Place in season, in place:
    crux of it, *cruz:*
    cave of the heart
        weevil:

    Why me, hackberry—
I am your friend. One song
    per season. Throw of
    yucca seeds lacquer black
        comes up

    Cool wonder of
All lives: one song per:
    Zebra swallowtail
        touch down,
        confer.

SOLSTICE LETTER

for Ray and Betsi DiPalma

I think of you
as the tarts come out
of the oven—Ohio butternuts
from Ohio butternut
trees—and last summer's
ash seeds rattle
in the wind beyond
the window: small
bat-of-the-eye pleasures
of winter. Deep. Distilled.
Discardable. Like frying potatoes
near the solstice (a big batch,
the Main Course, silverdollars
with onion flashed
to chestnut); Scotch,
no rocks; and travelessness,
the art of going nowhere
for a month or two.
           Last May
we drove to Arizona, sent
a paper plane down Canyon
de Chelly and spent days
steeping in the Chiricahuas,
the border country
crawling with humming

and other birds. Those cool
unsuspected canyons
tucked high above
the desert, the stillness,
their poise will take your breath
away. Dawn and dusk
cool air flows up or down them
like a tide; the sycamores
sigh. And on through the umber
to El Paso and Juarez
for blankets—those shrimp
and calamari vendors with their tubs
of ice deserve
a hungry painter—and north
through the panhandle
and east across Kansas
(foaming with early peonies
and late lilacs), skirting
the Ozarks and dropping
into Kentucky for Burgoo,
to Ohio, where we were given
butternuts
Many Hours in the Cracking,
and back,
full of space and scattered barbecue
and ready for more
and more of the continent
slowly taking solid form
within.

But now in December
we have the travelessness,
the distillation, the stirring
and the basting, leaving
one's wandering figment to carry on,
miniature Tarzan/
Astaire hybrid always out there
in the nonvoluntary imagination,
On Duty, crossing
and recrossing, fresh towns
at daybreak, with no baggage:
just a golfball-size nugget
of good parmesan
to be grated over anything
and everything at all.

Nights I whistle him in
like a dawg.

And sundown today
 (I'll think of you
when those hens come out
of the oven), sundown
this year, you have *word,*
finally, and we have a sky
the color of milk
that blueberries
have been in; mountains
to the immediate west,

their pines in intricate silhouette
this time of day; and coffees,
hot coffees: the gentle Kona,
a rare New Guinea "A."

WATER AND SONG

for MR

An early sky still up
for grabs: Flock settles
on the chance-medley phrase
                    three from Plaquemines—
the lark beat, the plumber
in it.
        Plumbers see
what doctors used to: the cheese with one bite
missing on strange tables and the dead mouse
under the stairs: take their pay in water
then disappear.
                    Kachina repairmen
dress like chimney sweeps: backseats full of
feathers and weeds: take their pay in talk
about the weather and dance on.
                    This springlike
Fall a shift of hemispheres:
Great-trade-routes-in-the-wings
in the wind: Pearls for oysters: oils
for an autumn scene
where a million winesaps roll
to bins—
        (From rare earth
mostly—
        (*three from Plaquemines*

SPIRAL EDDY

A yellowlegs calls.
Tom wrote "I wake early and go for a walk
under the orange lights round about the time
the dew begins to freeze on the roofs
of parked cars." Mothertongue, I got home tired,
threw open the windows, put on motets of praise
and rejoicing and a pot of green chile.
Minutes later a woman walked by, harked, stopped,
came to attention gazing up at the sky:
Garlic twining the ineffable, Langue d'ail—
whose sunset falls
on cold November ponds: sheets of mango,
persimmon faintly lapping, steady, decent
on the soul: Spirals eddy: Yellowlegs call.

PROPOSED ELEGY
FOR HART CRANE

What a place for a garden,
pain like a pocketful of mints,
we live on each other.

As if an immigrant family crossed
some mysterious brightly colored bridge
and wandered into this lung-like valley
selling hot sandwiches and aerial photographs
of the Aztec dead we live on each other.

Nothing was planned without noise;
after dark the siren comes on in sheets,
she turns over loudly.
                        I think I could paint
when her back's turned.
                        Her back.

Or walk a little farther upstream
testing the furniture and the hair
in this area.
Yes it's a beautiful country,
flowerlike and huge, all the more graceful
when you consider it's rolling
and our many coffees rarely spill
but sometimes it takes itself away.

CRAYOLA DA GAMBA

Aspen leaves
the size of dimes—
as dimes: whippets
without the
within: Days heavy
on the trumpet
voluntary: Days
pitch black and maize.
I had a smooth yoyo
those colors once.
We're talking about the sun.

Mustard mare,
four girls in yellow on her—
They're talking about the sun.

"ALL IS WELL"

A small hawk in the apple tree.
Eating a favorite junco. Little John, he
of the dapper hood and
salmon flanks.
                    As for anything
involving two pianos, the Turkish twins,
the Pekinels,
are probably the way to go.

That little extra doubleyolk something
(which in the realm of mountains
you will find in the Spanish Peaks).

"All is well."
                    We haven't had fish
for breakfast since the hotel
in Skibbereen two years ago—
"Fried plaice" (to be speaking of
Speaking in Tongues).

Happy early morning tongues.
"I'll have the plaice. Fried."
Broad white tablecloth. Just outside
the River Ilen ran. Runs.

FROM THE ERSTWHILE
FORKS OF THE GRAND

A day gray enough
crickets start to play by noon,
then stop.
        The place
holds its geo-duende
despite the dam's erasure:
her swollen forks
still show
from high points,
their succulent coulees
brightening early this year
trickle from flirtatious
prairie roll to disappear
abruptly, prematurely
into the reservoir
whose waters chop
beneath a heavy-handed autumn
front
skiing in all day on
scathing wind
with just one thing
in mind: Clear the joint,
strip it

like the Khans—
                    but
Nothing Personal.

Along the bluffs
we find debris of snake nests
in the sand: signs
of scuffle and four-inch
infant rattlers
curled crisp in death writhe,
cold-blooded agony
snuffed by gull or crow
one sunny day—

    Where's mama?

I find one crushed flat
in the road, dry
as onionskin, perfect
instant corpus delecti
in mid-stride—blango—
but
    Nothing Personal.
Its tail has a tiny brittle tip
of stuff the color
of thumbnail. I bring it in
for no good reason
and put it in
my Yeats.

A shivering patch
of goldenrod sends
flash of yellow writing
tablets (Goldenrod brand)
from erstwhile Septembers
long since mossing
and dozing beneath some chilly
backwater bay,

and the wind has found
the chokecherry saplings
in a deep ravine
and works them from the top
down: their upper leaves
already burn
with eerie translucent ochre/
rosé
where robins are drunk
on the fruit glut
and visibly hiccoughing,

and Sages quake—
man sage, woman sage—
the two species amingle
on the hills,
        balm
to dissipate the notion
that the hideous
is the especially true:

sacred
but not too sacred
but sacred enough
and conveniently rampant,
it is here
to wipe the arse with
as well as cool the heart
with
and clear the mutual air.
Tons of it within an all-day view
is frankly reassuring,

but it is still August
despite the ashen sky
and all its icing on
the duende and there is
August work to do
from which we will not
be distracted
or blown,
in which we slice the cukes
and Walla Walla sweets
and pile them
in a yellow bowl
to cover with vinegar and water
and a slash
of sugar and set them off
for half a day
to sour up good

and plenty:
              Done: the 1987 cukes.
The 1987 Forks of the Grand River
coulee cukes. Done,
and none too soon this blatant
Summer's End
when all things start to stop,
then hurry.

PISS ANT AND PEONY

The word *peony*
like the word *firefly*
held so powerful a charge
for the Japanese
it was used in poems
sparingly, with great care

and Harry
was Thomas Eakins'
dog. He watched
the Philadelphia fireflies
from his stoop. His master
brought home one night
a new painting called
"Whistling for Plover."

Harry watched the dandelion
fluff
drift by with constant
wonder. (It slows
but never stops—

Whistling for plover.
Whistling for lover.
Whistling for peony—
Peony.

WINTERBERRY

for MCG

Mornings we think up
the Spotted Horse road:
January morning force majeur:
The Spotted Horse road a thousand miles
west in imaginary April, or July: sagehens
strutting slowly through the sage—
chay, chay—

think of it
isometrically, just so over breakfast,
two people thinking same place
the way others clink glasses: the hills,
the hens thinking water, highstepping down
from the sage hills, elbow
to elbow at the pool.

We think of it, hold it
just above our familial heads
while we look at the winterberry:
crooked sprigs stuck in a cutglass cruet,
hard red berries winterburned
and wrinkled on a muck-black twig,
charcoal and scarlet on a cold week
sere as desert.

(Middle of the night I awoke
thinking two things at once: grand aerial view
of nocturnal beech forests
still bearing flaxen winter leaves,
their noble continuum across
the eastern continent, beatific presence
interlaced as lace—and Toni
unheard of twenty years
slinking into an unspecified steakhouse
in a tight black dress.) The two things
at once.

Bipeds: We look
at the winterberry, sole color
of the January worth it, dry scorched red
like a crimson peppercorn on the mud-dark twig
and think, together, *ocotillo*
in bloom, the same twosome
eked brilliance next to nothing, scarlet fleck
on spider black—
Up lifted.

We see each other
winter through. Beeches
by moonlight / Sagehens in contourline—
chay, chay.
We are bipeds,
we think of two things at a time.

THE RIGHT TO DANCE

You may mother may I
                    in Wm. Bartram
the possibility of meeting strangers
                    deep in the forest
giving away fawnskins
                    of wild honey.

            *

(Big brown eyes:
                    Sleepy
little space-station town.

SONG

Remember
the marsh arabs,
reed canoes
through Euphrates
marshlands:

Living on fish,
reed houses afloat
on baled-reed islands:
Water people,

skew-o-morph:
cries of terns
sharp
through the headlands.

DAYS A YEAR

APRIL

Dogs have
what kids lost.
Roy has his skull bowl
of cottonwood flowers,
plush crimson and green
(the mother tree bobs
and sways in the wind
like grass in slow
water): food for soft
thought, and I've seen
that mud stuck in *that*
handlebar hole before:
fallen bike, falling bikes,
they go down like dominos
this time of year.
Osier the fearless
puts forth.

MAY

Blocks of May,
chunks of May in blocks
of ice. Strung. Pearlwise.

JUNE

Genus Day-o,
Species Halting Vernal,
the dog-eared: low clouds

collar the spruce, soggy grays
clash numbly with fierce new greens.
The apple boughs bow.

"We go out in the night and cut
young onions in the rainy darkness—"
Tu Fu and friend, that we.

We go. We went. We went
and built a *tinga*, then a *mole*,
pouring the cinnamon-chiles

from high above into hot fat.
That was days ago but pockets
of the nose still hang

about the house, low
along the walls and in the shamrocks.
We tap them when we find them,

break them out.

JULY

That new early light in the trees—
familiar face of a stranger, strange
look on the thin friend—it burnishes
the fuselage as all the leaves
show their light sides with something
like a roar: Now here is a sunrise
they will speak of many centuries
down the line.
                        It bronzes the harebells
and basks on a hypersqualid surf-rocked girl
in ersatz leopardskin dress asquat
on random church steps. She is money,
the huge stone wheel sort dragged by bullocks
as seen in Ripley's *Believe It or Not.*

It lights on a harebrain in fine black suit,
expounding. His mouth is open,
his zipper is three-quarters open.
He is change. He passes like a kidney stone.
He knows not the cool of the dirt
three or four inches down.
                        July '49,
the one of a kind: one of my aunts
piles her hair so high and rococo-deco
it snafued Vliet Street traffic in Milwaukee:
High heels stuck in syrupy asphalt:

I was tethered nearby
dressed like an organ grinder's monkey,
a roll of caps in my little gun.

Thick July darkening the sky
like many many flocks! Your flies
will be swatted and swept away
with sprigs of marjoram, your tea ceremony
performed on red pinto mules.

AUGUST
rams SEPTEMBER,

the cool nights jar.

OCTOBER

Deciduous man: hot soup:
your bowl has a box elder leaf
in it: your flag shows
purple asters by the bushel,
as in stars,
and the yellow of many schoolbuses
parked beyond a river.

NOVEMBER

Où il se nourrit
Larousse says
regarding the oriole—

the sweet reflexive
flexing, kneading, feeding,
luxuriantly plucking nuts
and berries with both hands
through a pastel cool
like this one—
           Flash
of mussels marinara
far from here
gleaming in shallows; river
of fish. Eels. Browsing, sifting,
shaking the vines—où *il* means
the world, its traction
and drive.
                Check the orchards'
pink, gray/pink.
                  Check the pines.

DECEMBER

Little
but a spray of alder
from that sea.

JANUARY

Time vines, time
blossoms—
          Proviso:
the flicker comes too.

FEBRUARY

Half moon,
half sky: harbingers,
true tidings, light bulbs
above the heads, memoranda
from dream to dream,
thing to thing—
                dispersed
by wind, spread via bird
droppings or in the cuffs
of ancillary man who
hardly even knows—

standing half a block aroma-
side of the hot chophouse
in brief blue snow.

MARCH

When the big snows go old dogs stagger from the
houses and re-sniff each inch of pale lawn, pondering
last fall's diluted spoor all morning, scanning the washed-out
leaf wrack, not missing a blade, in a kind of stiff-legged
nirvanic trance—
    Persian patterns, disappearing ink—
    and a hundred particolored crossbills swirl into the pines
along the ridge, still warm from the cornucopia . . .

UTE NOTE

What is
that river, does it
have a
name? No.

Interblossom
submontane
Ignacio's

one cool slice
of bunting song—
We take the music
and leave the rind.

He—a Ute
with foresight—
says Goodbye,
I will
see you again
some time.

DOLL'S EYES

True uncut Milk of Mary so hard
to come by: the rabbit's foot market
shot: no call for oriole nests
used or new.
What's left? Doll's eyes.
Doll's eyes.

Once or twice and for all
the tea in China down
the garden path round
Robin Hood's barn and into
the forest for the trees—

to show you these.

    Anyone once loved
still loved—
            Hollyhocks
open in the alleyways:
                      confectionery
colors: cherry, sweet-tooth pinks,
mallow yellow:
            soda pop colors,
sticky jube jube—
              But anyone
once loved, still loved.

from **PENSTEMON BEARINGS**

The Black Hills lie to in their roads.

    *

You (Hilda Doolittle)
will find Junegrass
skinny in the wind, boney
old grama ablow, and know

what to do: find the track
faint in cool sand
and think *Claro,*
largo, cross White River,

Cottonwood Creek, Hat
and Antelope Creeks
with swallows in their shores,
their gaunt millionaire

trees: scan
cut of the bank, layers
stacked for soothsayer,
see grouse go off—

wham—old bones amutter
in pale grass, eyes tearing
with wind, find the round place
where the round stones

stay and cottonwood buds
packed scarlet, dense as roe,
worn Slim Butte far to starboard,
her venerable molar wisdom

with a gap for the chaff to blow
through—*whaff*. You will follow
the draw—Bonnet or Antelope—
trees one by one at your sleeve,

the hawk-dark
deep in the box elder, see
mule deer scat neat in the grass
clean as bird's eggs

and know without asking,
kneel to the tough runt-roses
one hand high (and think
Paris) and from a rise

look far-off at their island
pines and the wind like wheelbirds
in them, and think *Paros*—
that kingfisher sky.

LINES IN THE MIDDLE OF MAY

Someone shot the Tongue River sign—
shot it full of .30-.30.
      I live in a town
birds fly
through and over. Sing to by happenstance.
Bread is baked.
     Great rivers stand by:

Assiniboia with heart of stone.
Moreau, two Plattes, Cimarron.
The Niobrara, curvaceous
as an ice age. The Wind, the Bighorn—

They say you can see your face in it.

I'm not sure what's going on.
But somebody creamed that Tongue River sign.
And doves love robinsong,
       sit listening.

ALLDAY PURCELL

Red church against blue sky, smoke
solfatara from the dreams of whistling
dervish: to escape the danger that the music

will seem to press toward any particular goal.
Starlings hunker at the chimney lip,
pigeons stupid enough to rely solely

on the sun. Brick red,
sky blue, honey for the rods
and cones. *All ages are contemporaneous*

honey for the bones—
Such that we feijoada in homage.
Such that one morning we were out

at daybreak, happened across foxes
prancing dalliance in the snow,
also red, also against weak blue sky—

Fox Red, Sky Blue—
Ah Henry
You'll never see seventeenhundred.

TULIP TREES

Plum leaves *hang*
in crescent quarter moons.
Chokecherries' *lift*
in russet overtones.

Hello from halfway up
the hill, October the endless,
stone in the ring.

I fished that "secret" grove
last week—I drove you by
there once, I think—where the creek
dives into heavy woods
and veers. A pretty morning
not much in the way of trout.
Yellow leaves twirled on the water.
I started out with a Dave's Hopper.
Later switched to a big hairy-black
cricket imitation. A curious flicker
watched it go from the branch above
as though he were about to shapeshift
into a kingfisher. Fishing
in an election Fall . . .
                 Flocks
of starlings loafing in treetops,

waiting for warm sun on the Day
of the Fingerling, like, somehow,
(something about that slack
expectant aggregate), a pack
of baboons around a savannah pool.

Walking out through crabbed and bent
box elders, I missed you all
of a sudden, miens and ways.
I miss the tulip trees
back there. Deities it seems
are landscapes, plowed under.

And I stopped to see D.W.
last month for several days.
We ate well,
and one night after dinner
went out along the river
and into the woods to listen
for owls in the lowlands.
Walking through the dark forest
half-drunk brought back
pleasant pointless memories.
The owls kept their distance,
but two long, unhurried
freight trains bayed
melodiously in the night,
echoing gently across the valley

as if in sway
with one another.
                    Later,
in bed upstairs in the big
Victorian, a deep, eiderdown
sense of the many moons,
many moonlights, the phototropic
after-hours.
                    Then brittle
tight-lipped autumn thunder.

GENTLE RAIN

"A gentle rain comes stealing up from the east."
Reading by the little lamp a grandfather I was born
too late to know read by.
He worked the land, loved the Emperor Concerto.
I think he'd like these Chinese lines.
"There comes a wind blowing from the south
that brushes the fields of new corn."

NIGHT SKY,
PAWNEE CREEK

Rigel leaves a ripple—
   otter
      through black water.

ODORATUM

This is the week the yellow currant blows.
Blows through the yellow downwind house
we had one spring, all the starboard windows
open day and night to let the fragrance in,
the place so full of sweetness
we thought it might explode.

PHOTO DROPPING FROM AN HERBAL

It must be Presque Isle,
from the rolled-up pants of it,
the sand stuck the length of the leg of it—

Presque Isle of the hungry storms.

First French word I ever heard.
Little-girl prints down the beach, four,
maybe five inches long,

blurry gulls above potato salad—
gulls soon demoted:
Turn to the terns:

A Caspian works,
shadowed by a gull, its oceanliner tones
against the dark lake,

Erie. The Voice-under Terra verbatim
of it: Chronological contours
demanding dialogue, ransom, repartee—

"I was fishing up that creek
the day FDR died. A country mailman
stopped and told me at the bridge."

Or (at a pile of brick rubble and daub)
"We heard some nice Fauré there once."
Murmur sustenant.

It's got to be Presque Isle,
from the Are we children, to never tire
of it, to go on and on about it,

to climb Cobbs Hill to see the blue
of the big lake (Ontario) beyond, true North,
to go half days out of our way
to eat at the Basque hotel,

mention that Christmas
up the Yellowstone with all the eagles
flying by, sit for a minute in the plaza
of a one-time Seneca town, listening?

"Keep talking," Mrs. Messina
the super on East 12th Street
liked to say.

OLD FRIEND ON THE
QUIET SIDE FAR AWAY

This morning orioles seemed to spark
from every tree: "spots before the eyes"
after restless sleep.

And then the mountains west
blinding with late June snow.

How is that sumo live oak outside
your corner window?

How are those marvelous blond hills
rolling down to the sea?

BLUE RIDGE:
STREAMS ARE ROARING

Morning in the shade
of a persimmon tree. Later, downstream
below a hornbeam. A shy man hollers
from across the valley.

Every other rhododendron flower holds
a tiny bee, just the way
each macaroni shell in pasta e fagioli
eventually holds a bean.

A little Italian goes well up here.
Latin, too—*castanea, ruficapilla, caroliniana:*
Paroles: Dogwood calls the catbirds.
Black cherry calls the blue.

A GROVE ON THE MUSSELSHELL

Thin, scattered, sparkling
in the sunbeams:
                    box turned upside
down and shaken:
                    six grapes, bread,
a plug of jerky
                    on spread green
kerchief.
            When I open the goat cheese
strong like carrion—two days plus
in the cooler—
                    donkeys downwind
look up and over:
            Whiff of wondrous
Brave new fungus.
                    The Musselshell
low and easy. Across the way
a worthy grove, half-leaved
(October).
            Harmonic grove
of the old school at full attention.
The central tree, the maharaj, ascends
in musclebound gradients of three, lightest,
suavest of veerings
                    through ganglion of all

possible design, on
to the freestyle-flamenco upper right
where the eye seems always to end—

flare
where a kestrel sat in the sun
just now—
           What dear von Bingen
might have called
                 a *mediator bough.*

   *

   Since I cut back
to birds and rivers, life is smooth,
days surer, words flow
                  (or seep),
it doesn't matter that much
anymore.
          The night before,
I noticed Painted Robe Creek
in the atlas,
           drove out early morning
for a look.
           Slim pickings at first,
a treeless bed, lank
soldierly hills. Pheasants
in the stubble. The word
"forsooth" was in my mouth.

But a few miles in
the road upstream turned south
and soon there were pines
on the slopes,
                 the bottom narrowed,
the edges roughened, the road
lost shape, not a soul
in sight.
            A threadbare pensive
storm-gray came plodding down the road,
and then a stately single file, the rest
of the remuda, wild, almost a carnivorous
look to their eye.
                      And that
was far enough. Ten miles up, or in.
Turned around and drove back
down.
           The place it meets the Musselshell
must be a pretty one:
                          Multiple
decades of the name-silt.
                             Some other year.
But the eye was cast,
                   penny-ante
valley salted
            with song.
I smuggled that load
            up the Painted Robe Road.

And many variations thereon.

*

The pace of time
once so slow, then so fast,
slows again: Coefficient

of River Friction
                    shallow water
over stones.
              The first bearer
of garlic to the northern mountains
a Basque, unknown, herder
in a wool coat
                    speaking the sweet
late-late Neanderthal.

    We—
the cryptojanitorial *We*—
cut back hard: Rivers and birds.

And I quote:
              "Tanager talked.
Talked and talked.
And the people liked what they heard."

THE MUSIC IT WAS SET TO

They found the spool of Time
they say, day before yesterday,
that great butte russet and bone
hours north, then east and off

against a blue-black sky
swarming with swallows,
a vortical city of swallows
swarming the cliffsides

and storm-purple sky—
and the music it was set to, the cries
of the birds stitched counterpoint
against the rumble of heat lightning

honeycombed with years, the place
at last, russet on bone, without even
a name, only a poem, a vortical
city of swallows and a poem.

AUGUST EVENING

When the bats
                show up
the words drop
                down to hide.

MORNING WITH CHOKECHERRIES

Douse them, wet
they shine like brilliant
caviar (dust devils whirling,
cranes circling, babies
laughing, halfmoon sailing,
ravens, old station wagons
circling and circling), set
them in the sun.

CONSTELLATION: "BREAD ALONE"

Last leaves falling by night,
on the sly, black and white,
back door, left to right
across an almond moon.

SALUTE:
ON PEOPLES CREEK

Where it softshoes out
from the inner Bear Paws
and morning glories twine
on the meadow man-sage
I stop this looker noon
to shave—dusty horseface
in the car mirror song sparrows
hum along to.

But it is more than we think:
not Ralph or Cornelius T.
or Orrin U Thant Peoples:
The Atsinas say long ago a wild colt
with human head was born
along this stream. They glimpsed him
now and then, called him *I nit'ē i*:
"Person," "The Person"
(the English version smudged it,
river jumping track).

Born and reared along this stream,
roamed it all his loversnuts life.

"And did those feet"
e pluribus unum?
                    Not that we inhabit

a deprived age.
              Not that we inhabit
an age at all—
              Switching deerflies
in the goldenrod
with a girlfaced blackbird
on his back.

SOMETHING FOR JOHN CLARE

Spiderwort, the begs-
to-be-said: Fat of the summer,
off at the crack of the fat
of the bat. A pair of grosbeaks
feed in a hackberry tree
so lost in it all they have
a sort of kundalini air.
Orioles prefer the goatsbeard.
We watch the slow horses trail
the way Baudelaire, a Frenchman
who followed you through,
watched the clouds: a file
of chestnuts and flashy bays plod
across a meadow, drift?
it seems like hours, head to tail
past a clutter of fallen cottonwoods,
disappear up a cool box elder draw.
Then we watch the clouds.

ROAN MOUNTAIN:
VIREOS SING FALLING WATER

Those men in the valley
shredding lilacs in full bloom—
a little *too* human?

Vireos sing falling water, steady
as yesterday's rain.
Swallowtails flit and sip
among the fancy poplar flowers

sixty feet up—somehow
like memory waltzing.
Did I ever actually know
a woman named Normandie Beach?

Abracadabra
sent off out over the mountains
to soften the blow.

AS THE SEAS RISE

Pick and shovel men, hands and knees,
unearth the wreckage of a foot-long model
"Old Ironsides" where it went down
beneath a certain small Ohio town.

FROM, THEIR CLOUDS

Old blue Fairlane up beside,
waiting at a stoplight no cars
pass through. We glance at each other,
both feeling mealy under the Empire.
Although.
From any Platonic dialogue we gather,
know, that *beauty as moment all kingfishers
fly as one*, at once, is merely
a matter of time-in-mind, sunlit volley
biding. Trees, their clouds, wind
licks, falls with autumn thick of things—
Wet nights. Fat stars. Crickets singing in jars.

MEAL FOR AN ANASAZI BOY

Cashews, shrimp
with lemons. Thick bacon,
the best you can buy,
coiled around a pile
of mashed potatoes,
Georgia-style tomato gravy
on the top . . . *Shoofly pie.*

NOTA BENE

A palm or scoop of swale, a dimple in the grassy hillside
brimfull of plum thicket, twenty by thirty feet oval, drawn to a
head by a sibling pair of slightly taller hackberries in the center:
the entire grove (the leaves only a faint guesswork green haze
behind) in full about-to-levitate blossom, outpouring, cumulus
Surge unto Curd dense as English pudding.

Will you marry me? Not forever.
A towhee sings high up.
A coyote naps within.

THE PENCIL

As the Irish call steady whiskey
and its hook "the Creature,"
capital *C*, this going out, going out
to write and see, we'll call
"the Pencil," capital *P*.

A swell of peaks, one of them
High Swan, High Swan
just in from where?

We watch the roads back down below—
piles of words like piles of stone.
Landscape with curds, then whey.

Carya, the hickory nut girl!

    Stray October day.

BALLAD EXPONENTIAL

for Jeffry Traphagan

Lost,
one melancholic Siamese cat—
answers to Guido.

Last seen
tiptoeing into cotton fields
near vernal Vernon, Texas,

hometown of Jack Teagarden
("Davenport Blues," "The Riverboat
Shuffle" and all that).

Off to start
a waif cult. Stay alive
on cockroaches and boll weevils.

Blamer
the other evening
waving off moths and talking
about the steerage,

epiphanies delayed,

about running as a boy
to the A&P store for milk

several times a week, or cheap steak
or a pot of honey, with robins

in the twilight trees,
and learning only
when he was something like twenty,
pants an inch or two too short,

that it stood for the Great Atlantic
and Pacific Tea Co.—how it
caught him strangely in the throat,

grown man,
as though he walked on
a map or a globe—

and later went to Newfoundland,
clearest of lights,
every village given up to cod,
handmade signs in every shop—

big platters of sounds
broiled under cracked pepper
and pale cheese.

And a few years later
Prince Rupert, on the other side,
"Halibut Capital of the World,"
brimmed with it, buckets and gurneys,

three meals a day, the smell
lapping in the streets—
and suddenly struck equilibrium:

Lullaby calm of A,
then P. Sweetened air. Began sleeping
like a baby. Yawned and said

Good night
and climbed the stair . . .

    So those are the oceans
and those are the quays, towns
bearing fish and a squeeze
of lemon.

And steady the shores
for Guido, triangulation
achieved, living on fat crickets
and weevils: Has pull

like the moon
over red dirt. Will no doubt
come running to "Chico,"
or "Bevo." Maybe even "Enrico."

from **FOUR POEMS REGARDING
"THE HORSES"**

Daybreak finds the horses
browsing in happy omnidirectional
agate-toned array.
                    (Smashed the windshield,
took the Dante. Nothing more,
just the Dante.

BALLAD CIRCUMSTANTIAL

Family of nine
seeks sleeping room—

close by cigarettes
and pawn, view alpine,
no lawn . . .

"Like walking on the Gobi"—

Mimi last night,
along the river with testimonial
toad. Met by chance
beside the old stock bridge

across the Platte
that led for years
from cattleyards on the west bank

up and oopsey-daisy
to slaughterhouses on the east.

Now both ends chopped
brusquely off, a weedy midair
midsentence look to it:
"Like walking on the—"

Cast-iron span
plank-lined and floored,
vague sleight-of-hand decor

above a decent run of river—
young trees and a few teal.
Cool evening coral

in the west,
plenty of what she called
the Clearance—the greatest
of plenty—and we agreed

the worst of late:
those Mayan boys
died on 287, a carful
up from deep Chiapas,

drove straight through, lost it
at yucca daybreak, rolled it over
just this side of the Cimarron.

Old 287. Mayan boys
in Kiowa country, sharp
as ice, blind as lightning.

Headed for Denver in hopes of clover.

   Oh Mimi
at the stockyard bridge—

pretty toad purring.
Long paisley dress

dragging through the gravel.
The night was chilly.
Ruby-coral in the west.

FODDERWING

Look at the cottonwoods'
pure Nijinsky. Deep December
you know they low, groan and wail, sing
in the night like the famous whales.

BALLAD ABSTRACT

Turn at the second honeysuckle—

What's a Yellow Cab doing
so far out on Powder River?

Chiller music, the young shrikes
on the schoolhouse roof.
Avocets in mudpuddles

cooling their feet
from the Great Sadness

and butterflies
down from the Moreau hills
on business, in and out

of the imaginary. The nighthawks
blasting in early evening sky
(Ancient Gladness),

and the thousand cranes
streaming in downriver, whuffle
of wings in the halfdark

with the comet called Hyakutake
up and to the right, just inches off
Ursa Major: Peerage of the Realm:

Telling Joe the other morning
(a platter of spätzle) about the day
the *Lermontov* sailed

from New York, a pretty Saturday
in late September twenty years ago,
we were off to Le Havre—

how four or five liners left at once,
backed into the Hudson and departed
the harbor in procession,

south along the coast together
for an hour, maybe two, then,

abruptly, the *Lermontov*
peeled off to the east (the others
all Caribbean bound), off

into the North Atlantic
with just the first notion of sundown
coming on, and the great surge

of wild intimidating beauty,
almost disbelief, at that unforeseen
moon-simple moment, *Ship to shore.*

And who could work that into an eau
de cologne? And what's a barber pole—that
prize-winning symbol of the sempiternal—

doing twirling so far out
on Powder River, with the days passing,
curlew after curlew, stamstammering boy

sunflower after sunflower?
Take the well-head road after crossing
the bridge, travel through the iron gate

on the paved road
that soon turns into a shell road
and proceed to the backside

of the island. Go right
at the third forsythia, left
at the yellow currant.

Watch the motions of the stars
and note which part of the sky
changes little during the night.

Then, in autumn, fly away far
from that unchanging group of stars.

LAST NIGHT WE SAW
AND HEARD MS. FLEMING

A morning nears zero
(Fahrenheit), snow on the ground
so tight the wild turkeys
won't drop down from their roosts,
we can spot a few of the flock
up in the pinto pines
where they mutter and wait.
Gemütlichkeit.

*

One note so tensile thin and high . . .

*

Lorena,
"Lorena" the song they banned
from campfires during the war
between the states—too sad,
the boys too sad, too sad
to fight, entire armies
sobbing on their knees.

A Zanesville girl!

Sleep, sleeep with three e's.

SO THEY SAY

Clinch River breeze sugared by honeysuckle:
Mead-speed—so they say. Even the vultures
sit resting in the soft May day.

WITH THE UNKNOWN
PAWNEE MASTER

On top of hill
chokecherry bushes bend
under not-fruit/not-yet
but blossom.

On top of hill
fresh dung of horses
and chokecherry bushes bent low
under brazen greensweet blossoms.

Hilltop sweet
with cherry blossom
and *fresh dung of horses,*
but—

On top of hill
cherry blossoms,
fresh dung of horses,
but

No horses.

DAMSELS

By the second day
we registered the damselflies
resting in the pines
just overhead,

felt the many eyes,
turned slowly in our chairs—
demoiselles resting
in an utter stillness
on every other cranny
or twig, every tree,
copper-carmine, blanched lapis,
tails hiked in the cool air.

And when the wind
quickened, the full armada dropped
in pure consensus
to perch tiptoe on the buds
of sage a foot above the ground
below, a shift unanimous
as leaves in gust—

then up, moments
later, back to the pines,
the very twig, back to the mind's

amino sky. The lacquer blue
dropped down to investigate
my watch.

Touch of a hair—
what can they weigh? moment
of the day. To meet the earth
so slightly. Needlepoint toes.

What can the hummingbirds think?

Inca piccolos.

TO A MAN WITH COLD-HEARTED CHILDREN

A foggy Sunday, not for long.
We raise a crooked spray of flowering almond
cut before the clouds came on.
It hosannahs the house, even the town,

and now we can see the pass
you'll be driving over just after noon.
We'll show you the sourwood trees
and where the red wolf ran by the door.

Later, high tea with Barsac
down under the sycamores. Cake,
pie, rhubarb clafouti. All, or some.
So long as it's under the sycamores.

FALLING FOLDS

From the knoll road we befriended
I tried to catch the pitch of osier
where it follows the stream, declines
in gentle falling folds—
tried the Mongol vermilion overset
with Prismacolor plum. Then sat down
and wondered who would ever notice.
The likes of you. And thought of the old phrasing
when posting a letter: to "write north,"
to "write west." To be safe, scratch in
a pair of hawks, lazybones
of childish curlicue above the skyline sage.
River head, river mouth, riverbed.
Writing east, then writing south.

LI PO SHOULD KNOW

Ten thousand down, buried
screaming in rubble, drowning
in mud. Hills burst open, roads
from Chengdu to Wenchuan cut off
by landslides. Pandas
always the first to forgive
moan in the night.

May 12, 2008

MORE ON THE ROAN

for Martha Uchino

Vaudeville from the east,
farther east, Normandy, the Vau
de Vire, Vire River through Calvados
where the sassy songs dangle
from its trees.

The coffee is slow today,
no laughing matter. And you are off,
expatriating to Japan, this very moment
I believe, flying west to gain the Far East,
wherever you are, whatever day
and time you're passing through.

Fine flecks of roan
blow out of the north to season
the March gray. *Roan beauty*
sparking, of course, "Rome Beauty,"
two or three showing a spit shine
at rest on an old plate with paring knife,
a groundling still life
from an undetermined century,
undated and unsigned.

RED HILLS

Sienna, shades of soft brick,
one-time adobe, menudo
a day late set out in the hills
for Coyote—sienna *pobre*.

Puffs of seed
on the wind—the willows
wander.

    *

Lone world,
the rhymes with time—

Carmine the red
of the bunting breast
off in the hills' day,

hills the cedars climb,
burnt carmine.

    *

Red sky at night—fan dancers'
delight. Willows wander hands

in the air. A lien
on the *sanguin*, lean *sanguin*.

The hill willows wander years
from here.

TRAVELER'S TUNE

The *Lachrimae*, haven't heard
them in years. Years
and years. "Seaven Teares."
And then we hit the mockingbird.

UNDANCEABLE

1.

Wisha, the women
were singing, the song
carried on the air,

moved and melted
down the valley: a place
in-velvet

like an elk: then
the sparrows new-to-
science picked it up

from the yucca stalks,
the songs in tandem
filled the bottoms

like a day (we knew
in a waking world it was
Tongue River with chicory

and the sparrows were
breweri—but *Thoughts of you
looked our way.*

2.

Some days wanting gulls
below. Three roans in the shallows,
one of them blue.

We held to prehistoric routes
still kicking: smoothworn edges
over easy: "Crow Ford"
to the Yellowstone . . .

The pretty lancehead found
among the cactus flowers by one of those
for whom it was originally honed:
That hillside has a sense of humor.

Kingbird gambit, kingbird rules.

. 3 .

Dauber swallows build their town
no hands. Two thousand trips
to the mudhole.

"This is where they bring the senators
to fast naked in the muck, wail
for prudence from the sucker fin."

We meant to stop and paint
the old hotels fronting the tracks
in Poplar, get the distant river trees
reflected in the dusty glass,

but it was Thursday, and we
were Sunday painters, by then
we were facing the Killdeer range—

And everywhere the million sunflowers
gazing.

4.

That was Old Woman Creek
caught your eye, the staggered
falling fifths a surprise
distaff in the basso.
A rough night, compañero.
One spotty fawn dead
on the centerstripe, several
nighthawks also down.
Then we were behind a man
in a daffodil Olds whose ears
stuck out in silhouette against
the plains, way out, just like
a lad I knew in school
days. He could touch his tongue
to the tip of his nose
no hands. Mimicked ominous
distant thunder from the back
of the study halls. We envied
his idiolect and his rumpled look.
Some of us suspected he had
connections with the Kinsey book.
Could it be? Way out on Old Woman Creek?
We followed him in duple time
from Red Bird to Jay Em.

5.

Since you asked:
It is a pomander:
But this is not a moral tract.

Please find enclosed:
one sun-dried male yellow-head
from the berm of the Mahto road.

6.

You know those breaks west
from Cut Meat . . .
                              ! Take it all
by night, run it by moonlight
and moonlight only

for a week, Moonshell valley
and the Moreau with the top down
four a.m., sidereal bareback, miles

of Sandhills by lightning strike
white as day, Taurus
and the little Sisters, three roans

pure chiaroscuro, lunar buttes
and night sage in the head,
locking down at daybreak, blinds

drawn tight, then out again
with poor-wills at darkfall,
Sweetgrass Hills, the Bear Paws

whose Milky Way—

7.

Further instigations
            from Ancient Wisdoms
transcribed in the form
            of a waltz.

ROMANIAN ELEGY

for the trampled of May '44

Tipilesti, Crivesti, Tautesti:
Horlesti, Halancesti, Falesti:

Barbotesti, Dumesti, Costesti:
Harmanesti, Negresti, Barlicesti:

Timicesti, Stornesti, Sinesti:
On the chance that memory

stands *out*side, like lichen
on the bark of a tree.

SCUPPERNONG

Scuppernong and *crupper*—wickets
to the dead, bright butter on stout
black bread. Boil the crupper seven hours
with sea salt and onion. Watch the days
cook away while the nights dive,
hive dark firefly jelly, recombine.
Like corn-stripping time at old Hopewell—

    Child Carol that May
    as the swarm of birds
    tumbled through the lilacs
    in the park—Blackburnian,
    palm, redstarts, black-throated
    blues—"Do they have a heart?"

BARTER: IDLE THOUGHTS OF BODMER

After the razorback hills
the buttery bottomlands.
Look at the avocets,
no one you know,
napping like flamingoes
on a secret sand bar
in the Moreau.

After the buttery bottomlands
the pine-faced hills.
Look at Deers Ears
vague as Venus
forty solid miles to the south.
In the box elder breaks a secret cuckoo
calls with a luna in its mouth.

THREE SETTINGS

1.

ALL SOULS

Hermaphrodite Creek,
44 N   101 W.

The people are friendly,
the coffee is sweet.

2.

A RANGE

A bank (like evening clouds)
of old-time toy soldiers
chipped and gouged
blind baby-doll eyes,
red rosebud lips.

3.

O, THAT MUST HAVE BEEN

Otter, upper Otter,
pinyon jays deploying
from the morning hills,

cries so sharp, so carefree lost
in curve of the earth and constellation—
as if the cedars sang.

CONSTELLATION:
"THE TENNESSEE WALTZ"

So named
because when watching these stars
you soon hear the rustle
of roadhouse wind, and then
the thin violins.

WALKING WITH CHEESE

in memory of Michael Gizzi

Last week that knob of aged Cantal
moved along the Quai d'Orsay
in Ronna's purse like a crumb of supernatural
cake, across three bridges and Île Saint-Louis.
You might have tracked it on a gifted radar screen.

Sunday,
Rocamadour in the style of a coin
went with us through the caged-bird market
Place Louis-Lépine.
Fancy finches sensed it and began to sing.

And for the Rilke walk
we chose the Trou du Cru, the inch-and-a-half
heart of the Époisses, chose it over the Reblochon
and slipped it in the pants to troll and trace
his path of 1907 when he was off
most every day for weeks to see the Cézannes
just up in the Grand Palais.
Walking in footsteps, bearing cheese,
from dove-colored 29 rue Cassette, his rooms,
north in the shadows to rue de Rennes, la vie
Mansard, to Boulevard Saint-Germain,
white buildings and red geraniums,
across a bridge, a light chop on the Seine,

then a hard left at the Place de la Concorde,
at the hieroglyphs, and along the balustrade—
a pair of yews!—to the steps of the palace
and its statuary, where Rilke stood looking
for days at the paintings from Aix, steeping,
cracking the code, and the letters he wrote
late afternoons . . . And finally the token cheese
just in from Burgundy, as gendarmes watch:
Pull it in half and squeeze it gently on the bread.

After that it was music, or the thought
of music more than words, the token cheese
the human honey more than words
that led us on a Friday with frets
on its neck through the Luxembourgs
past all the queens of France with a wedge
of Saint-Nectaire in the jacket (carried
like a tune) to Avenue Gay-Lussac and down
rue Saint-Jacques to number 269,
the Schola Cantorum, where a few late
butter-colored hollyhocks bloomed
in the courtyard with its footsteps
and tracery of Roussel, D'Indy, Messiaen, Satie.
But the cheese is for Joe Canteloube,
the *Chants* from his native Auvergne,
those soprano high notes soaring and sailing
like a flamingo up the Rhone. A piano chords
from the back, a violin unlimbers
in a curtained room.

Now these October days seem miles
apart, half-sunny days with a dusting of sea salt—
or is it small gulls? The news seeps in
one *porte* and out another, bad news
from the west this week, and our tough crottin,
vest pocket left, we smell it as we stroll, a nose
like most every sweet-dream mud-pie
chestnut-leaf terrine you've ever seen, down
the Boulevard Saint-Michel, sad today, Michel,
sad shoes, sad plaid, sad cheese the human honey,
and a wild "Bailèro" blows by heart
through the trees where gargoyles perch
and preen and crane to see.

October 2010

TWO HAWKS

Two hawks
in honeyed circles interlocked
on the one thought.

SONG NEAR NO HEART

Left hand in front, fingers
upward, bunched as a kind of bud,

then the right, closed gently
around them just below the tips:

a band, of people, bound, moving
through the days and nights.

ALL ALONG

Ronna
in the yard, laughing
like a wood thrush.

Orioles would take
this long blond hair
on the boudoir sink.

ON A PHRASE FROM
THE CONFUCIAN ODES

    Chalcedony
and the cheese resembling chalcedony.
The first generation sold the stone.
The second the cheese resembling the stone . . .

    By orioles I mean
those who harbor seasons
unseen: Upstream, downstream,
familial as hail or night rain.

Who pack them
as continuo, sing welcome
far in advance: Worn shoes,
orange pants.

Who name the tree in the town
where waxwings rested
last year, year before: Held, ancestral
as Maydew. Flock perpetually

touching down.

BULL RUN IN OCTOBER

1.

Lone persimmon,
Matthews Hill:
                    Diospyros
on a low Virginia knoll:
                                Diospyros
virginiana,
                fruit bright high
in the crown.

When the lecture group leaves
I'll toss a stick and knock some down

(VMI boys, that's my guess, and professor
in Kazootie ballcap
                        over by the Union guns).

    Meanwhile
resting in its spindly lee.

    Dios/pyros—
food for (smooth) (Virginia) gods.

        *

Dense woods to the nearby east,
burly edge just reddening.

Pie-eyed shitepoke
(euphemistic wonder of the world) flaps
along the run; the run and hay fields
on the side hills steam in morning chill.

Dogwood plum, sour gum claret.

Tang of green black walnuts on the air.

Jays steadily
over and back
across the stream—ferrying—
with acorns in their mouths.

Smilax, odor of fox.

"Southern Serves the South."

*

October.
                The great forest
suspensory.
                Not July.
Flame lowered.
                Cut bells.

Rumors of dancing at the fall line.

(You can see the Blue Ridge,
Signatory,
beyond the tail fins
from Dulles International,

some of these calico hills.)

*

Bull Run rises
in mountains of the name,
makes southeasterly

for the bay—
Occoquan, then Potomac—
maybe ten yards wide,

laggard with fallen trees
and mucky islands, flood debris,
motion imperceptible

except for leaves along
for the ride. On the quiet side,
like your cousin's anaconda.

Thinks bay, knows highlands.
Piedmont bluebirds overhead and all
those colored pencils in your pocket.

Fits in the palm of a hand.

*

The Domain: Oak-Hickory:
Mesh, chain, and law
just short of metal-strong.

Pale asters tremble in the understory.

Oddest of dimensions and calls.

Long lazy fly ball to left center.

Hardly memory,
                barely fact.

Excursion to hear an ocean.
                            A formality,
with parasol—
                hill, dale, hill—
a tense reserved
                for the sea.

        *

The thrushes a multiple.

Hickories a multiple,
                        staunch multiple
just short of steel—

shagbark, shellbark, mockernut,
pig.

    But the oaks—
the oaks alone can timber a world,
stave one:

Chinkapin. Red and post.
Chestnut and overcup. Blackjack
and bluejack.
                Bear, willow,
water. Turkey, scarlet, possum.
Black, shingle, pin.

They rustle and groan:

The Oaks:
        Comfort of cohort:

No lone persimmon.
            No single thing.

2.

Chinn Ridge.

Pines
just short of sway
above the oaks.

Pines like palms.

"We live in cloudy times"—

Mr. Hans Neuberger,
who studied the skies depicted
in six thousand paintings,
1400 to 1960.

"Increasing cloudiness"

he said,
peaking in the 19th Century
then tapering from 1850—

but skies never quite so blue
as early days.

*

In a shadow
or a lee.

Blue beech suddenly
by virtue of its portion
and knuckled grace
a favored tree.

That scrapple was good
this morning, lettuce
and tomato. I wonder
what it is exactly.

The freight trains
past the fleabag in Manassas
every twenty minutes
were troublesome at first

till I remembered tracks
and trains, those very
tracks, beyond the wren,
brought the day on,

nailed the place.

Sit.
Warty groundling apple.
Advanced chromomania
and a love of maps.

*

One redbird from the right,
through welcome Nameless Clearing.

Any bird from that side
bodes well
according to the augurs.

Augury an art to spell
the neck from craning ever backwards.

Welcome pause of Nameless Clearing.
Aroma of cedar, mycelium, and what we used
to call "fishworms."

A stand, or band, of Indian grass
footsure, forthright unto delegation,

Declaration,
and the scent of the cut-hay meadow
carries into the adjoining woods,

mingles with cider-sweet forest floor.
Tulip tree. Shinny up,
have a look around.

Southern Serves the Fragrant South.

*

Just being near the Capital
makes me nervous now and then.
Eight or nine leagues—
slip away, back into the trees—
as the blow flies.

Rappahannock, Mattaponi, Rapidan . . .

Hard smash to deep right.
Carney covey call.
Deck of cards, pack of hounds.
Greasy Van Dyke. Sticky summer night
with running lights.

"What did you say you're doing Halloween?"

*

 And the way,
as a boy, I was taken
with groups and simple constellation—
collections of leaves, butterflies,

sets of coins, fleets, fifty buckeyes
in a tray—
   contingents—
I read the names today:

 The 1st Minnesota,
the 2nd New Hampshire, 4th South Carolina,

8th Georgia, the 11th Indiana Zouaves,
14th Brooklyn, 4th Alabama
and the 3rd Maine.

2nd Wisconsin, the 1st Rhode Island,
4th Alabama, 2nd Ohio, 8th Georgia
and the 3rd Maine.

        Cohorts.
            Brainchild.

No single stranded thing.

3 .

Early morning, 39 degrees.
Silly songs running through the head.
Red vines wound high in the pignut leaves.

Crows far off in woods to the north,
equally, identically, excited
again today. There was a minor

fashion shoot
on Henry Hill last afternoon—
ankle-length black lace cardigan,

striped shaved-pony-hair chacha pants,
head cocked against a tree. Low sun
beaming smoky pools. More soon.

        *

Bull Run Stone and Gravel trucks
blow by ten times a day along the Sudley Road.

    "The Quarriers."
    A set.

Red vines high in the pignuts—
Mace on nutmeg.

Scrapple: minced pork in spicy cornmeal mush,
set up, sliced, fried upon a stove.

    *

    Chinn Ridge.
    Farewell.

Straycat breeze just short of chop.
Pastures groomed and held
against the insatiable oaks.

Hard little sugar pears
from feral trees along one edge.
I'll take some for the trip.

Songs silly
through the head—

"Her name,
her name, I swear,
was Sylva Looney."

Muttered near a rail fence.

And then
over by the drive
another persimmon—

back near
the 5th Maine
("I hated to kill those brave men")
battery.

A twenty-foot tree,
fruit dead ripe, spindly lee.

Peace to the Skinny and the Sent.

*

Dead soggy ripe,
the size of a jawbreaker,
radiant coalbank-furnace orange.

Sepal remnant humble cruciform,
botanical sonatina.

Inner pulp brilliant
equatorial sundown mash.

Four flat off-round seeds
roughly the dimensions of
a tiddlywink winker

in a sort of brilliant stack.

(Those pretty oyster shells,
half a dozen from the bay,
in an old farm dump beside the trail,
licked very clean—
"We share molluscan days.")

Lone persimmon,
                    thrush
to sing.
            Diospyros
sticky on the hands and face.

No single stranded cut-off thing.

from **TUNES MEANT FOR WHISTLING**

A GLOSS

Sometimes the dreams wander off
across the bridge and south, farther south,
where wild plums hang on the limbs
all winter long. *Chanteleuserie,*
the place where they sing, steelweed flowers
cold to the touch, the atlatl with ribbons
beneath a Christmas tree.

A SONG

Born to bees (they follow the deer trails
down to drink from the rivers).
Born to crows' eyes
the furnace-red of sunrise,
and a country girl, old mosquito bites
up one arm and down the other.
Born to Draco, low,
or the lights of town, or home,
or cooking fires off along the mesa—
Lost Horizon in a common poem.

WALKING WITH JOE

We stopped at the pond
when it reached the full peach
of the lower sky and the sudden silence.
Gentle ringlets began to show
on the still water. Here. There. There.
Quiet dimples, soft pocks and their halos
in hiding across the cool pastels.
"The haiku are rising."

NOT SO FAR UPSTREAM

The lights of Like-a-Fishhook
so hard to read by, like a woman
or a man in the morning, morning
after morning, and the lay of the land
and what's on the river today—
Miraculous mergansers. Stilton, with honey.
Rembrandt's rain upper left, fine
parallel sepia lines curling to filigree.

A VASE

Witch-hazel time. Waverly Place.
Garrets still the rage.
Out the window a Tree of Heaven
or two, then the Women's Prison,
points north up the avenue.
Poems rustle in occasional breeze.
Years numbered from the birth
of Christ. But the words
were saying, "*Vireo*—I am green,
green with it, spathe and seiche.
Down of your down, lace
of your lace."

WHEN THE THRUSHES
COME THROUGH

As great a pleasure of late
forgetting the fancy words
as it was to learn them
far back in the first place . . .
When the thrushes come through
fat persimmons let go,
tumble down the quiet days.
Walnuts splash in the spent rivers—
horses look up. Winds die,
and the nights make way.

TO PARLAY

Born to parlay "First yellow leaves
on the ash trees / Cool breeze up
the backside / Spinach to Popeye."
Born to wash, wash and dry
the hand-me-down stone axehead bashed
by ploughshares, blistered by centuries.
Born to call the dog Houdini.

FOR A MAN JUST IN
FROM MONTANA

To me that sounds like
Ermine Mountain—white all winter,
sorrel-horse brown in summertime.

*

As if by seashore fireside.
Memory the distant cricket.
Washes her hands of it.

ANOTHER PLACE

Another place I wish you knew,
that elemental cove
where the beeches hang low
over the lake, and with a skiff
or a canoe we could sidle in,
sidle under for an hour, coaxing
the little nuts from the limbs
into a hamper or a hat,
elemental hour, its drowsy
disembodied sounds and gold-leaf,
then drift back in toward town.

NOWADAYS

Nowadays
the good birds dodge the capital,
cut to Shenandoah, or the Chesapeake,
plying the penumbra, the underside
of the leaf where the soft songs
and the nearly-never-known
take hold and ride.

AESOP AND ISSA

Fausses Grives: This will win you
a woman or a man, this pork liver
49 cents the pound, sliced thin,
rolled around juniper berries
and wrapped with bacon, tied
with string, then simmered with garlic
in May wine. Half an hour after—
your six little thrushes to sing!

CANTU (AS EVER)

Forsythia time, cold calico
below. Pines bobbing cloudy green
on the gray bay of deciduous barrens.
So little. But a little. And the basso the basso
of the groaning earth. The baritone
the baritone of cattle lowing. The tenor
the sheep and the *tantes* and the *oncles*,
the tasso and wind in the firs.
Contralto the whisper of heat lightning
and shepherds singing to their herds.

RABBIT MOUNTAIN

A funny place,
faint echo of a pine, Rabbit Mountain,
to think of you:

Young Vogelsang,
at 3rd, blond curls, gloved hand
outstretched
imploring.
(An umpire.)

Aw your old man
never saw September.

Shrimp-fed boy.

Still a most timeless of
compliments: "You smell like
a prairie fire."

In that era
we chose our friends by their ability
to imitate animal calls.

(Split a Lucky Strike,
took to the rhododendron dog-breath
roads—never met again—

      (Passed the same
Chronicle stand each or every
other day:

                  (*DACCA TEETERS.*
DACCA TOTTERS.
                       DACCA FALLS.

A NAP BY THE KICKAPOO

What a face
on that barred owl
dead beside the road—

Rolled it over to see.
Round, jolly, cowled. Lightly
concentrically ringed.

The calm cosmonautical
with the simian fey.
                            Fox sparrows
sing. "We hated to be apart.

Even for five minutes."
The dreams come down—
Extra! Extra!—

from the cedared hills
across scant pasture
and April brambles

to the leaky
treehouse on the knoll
beyond the stream.

from **UNA DOZZINA**

Code name *Fava:*
an hour of April snow
from Sansepolcro
quarter, swirling down
the hills, and then
back up.

Shaggy bluffs: long-legged bird:
A man plowing.

What is the verb?

          *

Each morning
up and down the valley
smoke from various fires
(burning off the olive prunings)

curls and plumes,
leaning with the day's breeze.
Mountain people along

mountain roads bend
cutting wild greens.
They carry something

like a civilized
machete. Five minutes of
dancing hail. The dog

runs round and round
the house. Step outside
each evening

in hopes of nightingale.

 *

That battleground
where Hannibal fought
down near Tuoro—
Fat cattle wearing bells
laze around

just as you might have thought.

And St. Margherita's mummy
high on top Cortona's hill.

Her view. Her plan.
Her viewability.

We think of her from miles away,
her little fingers like burnt bamboo.

 *

Although
Solvitur ambulando
and *Fex urbis*
lex orbis most all my Latin

of any use.
To market for cheese, hat
and chard, eel.

     *

And the sea
with Elba rough and dark
and Montecristo
moreso. Red poppies
and bees. You
would think,

standing beside it,

"Tyrrhenian"
and "Mediterranean"
shot from the same
stock.

Apparently not.

     *

Coastal pines
from above resemble clouds
from below, as Percy Shelley
would well know,

as the redbuds
in Siena's hills the other day
did spring mornings,

Virginia mountains
the third or fourth
of May.

To be equidistant: the verb.

*

And a man came down
the beach
one hand pulling a stout line
stretching far into the surf,

with something on the other end
like fish or several seals
on a leash, it seemed

to ride the waves,
then came back the other way
half an hour later, tether

in the left hand now, now
it appeared inanimate,

a "sled," or drag,
a "sea sled"—an old Etruscan
isometric? He wouldn't say.

AN ANN ARBOR MEMORY

for David Cooper

Like eohippus.

Those long Novembers had some April
in them. We were standing
on a quintessential street corner, under
an iron lamppost, books heavy in the hands:

Elm leaves crunched (soaked,
then frozen overnight) in the gutter.
And the day had slumgullion at the end of it
with Alfred Deller on the side.

The way the preposterous mingled
so fluidly with the sublime: weird caporal
and instant coffee intertwined. "I'm color-blind
and I'm looking for a house with a red door."

The Blue Front beckoned,
Cadillac under snow beckoned, and Yellowknife
via the Cartography lab.
                              A runty eohippus
on a distant hill. (Below,

a scraggly circus crawls through town:
six bleary cars and weary trucks

with hula skirts and pythons in the trunks,
dreary morning verge of rain:

the grand *aiee:* Flag it, paint it, hail it,
at least slow it down. "Now, lad,
it's just a scrawny circus leaving town.")
The shiftless Huron flowed. Green cardamom,

black cardamom, and the cumulus code
was broken, message received: Great boulevards
with alleys and monkeys in the Brie.
Perfect cobbles rolled by perfect seas.

SYSTOLE VARIATIONS

The straits of July.

A strange moth in the keyhole.

The summer deep
as of piles or hills
of leaves or snow.

Bring it over
through the solid month
that mouse-colored horse
you wish to sell.

*

Over
with your train of jays—

That love once-removed,
numb,
like a leg or an arm "asleep."

Should they go up after
all those frozen bodies on K-2?
Or no?

The ritual feint,
quick tally of the joule.

With your big tonnarelli,
tadpoles in your pools.

    *

Where bark has fallen
the inner lining hangs,
frays to supple honey-beige,

could pass for
ribbon by night:

Come over with your
jays and your tagliatelle,
through the solid week
to the warm day:

Closed,
then suddenly open

like the eyes of a child
at first light.

NIGHT TRAIN

Head against the window
you could read the season even
through the darkness. Fat barns,
mist and bales. Foxes tiptoeing
the fencerows.

Wandering seasonal workers in old China
were known as "sparrows."
That lad in shackles being led
to the gare, Auxerre, way back there,
head so low, still brings tears.

The slow coal-black hills
of Pennsylvania, hawks on their mountain.
A seafood truck full of ice
in the tick-tock lights of a crossing.

Head against the window.
That holloway, love-of-my-life, near Selborne
a dry river now, trace and trail
of uncountable souls, souls
with feet, and even shoes. What more proof
do you need? To see it from the moon?

The Voice of Things
almost put me to sleep . . .

How I remember his fine black suit
and starched white shirt
when he came to read in Ann Arbor!

I scribbled on a pocket scrap,
yet again, "Scrolls September rolls,"
and then New York, dirty dawn, rumor of rain.
(Gloria Swanson was on that train.)

BLACK COVE:
THE NANTAHALAS

Midnight cove
with blue gentians in its folds.

Birds talk softly in their sleep
as this poem talks in mine.

Black cove, wet gentians ankle-high
by weak starlight—

Locus ceruleus:
dark, gentian-blue
place in the mind.

THE BARK OF THE DOG

Tercel, impending, lean
palette of the pintos—

falcon-gentle, queen
of warm meadows, impearling—

What's that song?
"The Bark of the Dog."

Lord, that woman's room
was clean.

*

Pale, down through love grass,
elegant as shell—

down from the memory hills,

one bearing melon,
one bearing cream.

*

Love grass, *Eragrostis*,
waving by the roads—

full-summer recalibrated
mandala-haze.

We slept in the attic,
made young love one morning.

The old farmhouse shook,
dishes in the sink

gave way. We heard later,
in town, it was a small-scale

quake. But those
were well-connected days.

     *

One with tamarind honey, one
bearing sweetest of creams.

O-he-ho. "Great River."

Eye of the deer,
sticky summer nights—

fireflies,
the great moundbuilder
mounds to the south

under moundbuilder dew—
mandalic pedigree.

I rarely thought of them
then, but I think

of them now.

    *

One with tamarind honey,
almond eyes.

Your face came clear
the first time in years:

tête-bêche.

Yes moonlight.
Yes starlight.

Sleeping Bear white
in the night—

blancmange.

*

So shy of the long dead:
heart-tied. No more:

down through dunes,
down through moonshed,

deer trail thin on the ground.
Honeyed melon—

ocean egging on.

*

Young birds in nest
know it best—

tanager tongue—

one in falcon colors,
cinnamon teal

(the great river effigies
wingspread by night to north
and west, watermark and cachet).

One with ready summer brie—

shell, far inland,
beads from the sea.

*

Waves of love grass,
bobbing, nodding—

These memories make me
drive too fast. Three
tickets in two days—

Plea the love-grass plea.

*

We hardly knew.

Falcons-gently, one
Mother-of-Pearl—

We hardly knew
those shells were from a distant sea,

that such a sea
was even in the world.

HUNTER'S SKY

Beauty to Lovely, the three thin miles,
then turn around to do it again.
Birds flush up as leaves drop down.

Orange-gold trees hunched
against slate-gray clouds: a hunter's sky.
The little road goes round the hills,

over and back like a jump-rope song.
Crows the birds of paradise sail by.

A *TAZZA* FOR RAY

Triste trafic—

Tine-heavy forks
cast by a chopstick people.

Then ah!
the old Monongahela favorite,
peanut butter on young beech leaves.

    *

April coals to April Newcastle.
All those thousand letters shuffled,
packed, tied tight with celery string.
They swing from the vines,

sad, said,
a little red that howls
a rest from the goose-turd green.

    *

Said sad postman still whistling
his way down sunny Walnut Street
 (Hello, Ed. Hello, Beryl)
with your laugh in his pack.

Warm music.
Warm music sight unseen
in the wake of fifty-year renga—

that blackpoll tiptop the maple
sweeter than mail.

AN ENGLISH POEM

Jackdaws
Stonehenge northeast portal lintel
born and raised: lens where landscape
drifts to tumble, always landing
on its feet.

Two weeks
without garlic, weeks with sheep
on every meadow, every hill
and Langdale. Fox fern the color
of chanterelle,

and then
the fox, the proper, dead along
a Dentdale lane. Someone tossed it
on a haystack in the sun,
a circumstance

we were meant
to merely graze. The Swale
the color of strong tea
with a pretty pearmain polished
on the pants.

There's a place
just outside Selborne
in the trees—a perpendicular on a path—
where you can stand, if it's October,
and pull down

beechnuts
from limbs overhead and pluck
blackberries a long arm's length
on your left. That going down, over
the South Downs

to find
a swannery by the shore:
testy cobbs eye the Fleet. A wonder
soldiers didn't eat them all, back in
1943.

This troupe
of parakeets does a fine line dance.
High tide for the Thames. Mudlarks
are sleeping. Mudlarks are sleeping.
God save the lens.

DICTUM

Poems
        like irises
rise
    to perpetuate their kind.

THE SERPENT

The English had a horn
they called the serpent—
a throaty bass
             that comes to mind
here,
     the mound
after many consultations
                  as much pure woodwind
as anything,
           high note held
over centuries
              with swallowtails
through it
          and *Myiarchus*
(the snake birds)
               in its tulip trees,

a tune you might whistle
              for someone antipodal
and wondering
             (passing through)
when the words tire
             and it is just pre-June,
just post-glamour,
             when only the cuckoos

and the yellowthroats sing,
                    stitch through the day,
the steady, all-summer songs,
                              unhurried,
unfooled.

        *

Best to begin
                    at the tail,
once you've verified
                    how the whole fits
so perfectly
                    along the spine
of the ridge
                    high above Brush Creek,
follows
          the quiet given curve—

at the tight coil of the tail,
                    the beginning,
the Great Plan conceived,
                              the talking
and the pointing,
                    laying on of hands,

and from that cochlea coil out
                    the creature flows,
labyrinth unfurled,

                    elegant as days,
spiral yielding wave,
                        gently leftward
with the given,
                    calculation held
in the clays,

culminating in the simple head,
                            schematic gape
with what is often called
                    an egg therein,
elongate oval
            at the very prow of the ridge,
sharp drop to the creek
                    below,

and on all sides
                the full forests
rise, maple, oak,
                    ash and tulip trees,
shadow languor,
                a moist breeze—
the snake bird runs it—
                    wheeep.

    *

    One day as a boy
    I saw the Seip Mound

                    to the near northeast
under brand new snow
                    with already a garnish
of sledding tracks
                    down the slope
and zagged paths
                    back to the top
and knew that that
                    was fitting and proper.

But the kinetics here—
                    less for the viscera
than for the inner ear.
                    Best to walk it
from the tail out,
                    walk through the form,
orphan Unearthly
                    rendered Earthly,
the low note held
                    by sun on stone.

And the simple sweetness of it
                    in the end,
compared to something
                    like the Sphinx
gnawed desert bone,
                    scorched sand
versus cool loam,
                    sugar of sugar maple.

*

From the center
        of the oval
a redbud grows
        and a bluejay paused,
homage-fire in its eye
        and a tiny egg
in its beak
        dripping bright yolk
dandelion—

        The early English
had a horn.
        E-I-E-I-O.
Cuckoo bird
        and red wren.
Templet and Mend.
        From the shade
I hear it as
        a whistled tune
of arms-in-bridge,
        a tune for siding with,
for standing up and siding with
        the sun,

that seamless fit,
        daily sidereal
on the sycamores—

Trajectory mend
of lover's intent—
　　　　the Caliber
and the Carriage of it.

The Serpent Mound
Adams County, Ohio

CONSTELLATION:
"FOX AND GEESE"

Near "Flies,"
just east of "Sleep"
(as in the bits of amber
that gather overnight in corners
of the children's eyes).

THE ROAD TO HI HAT

Sunrise hurt the cat-owl's eyes.
Crows go to ground in the slim valley.
Past Hard Shell, around through Softshell's
barnless swallows.

Transhumance
older than the hills: Up the mountain
in May to see the spindly sourwood flowers.
Down in the fall with the firelit honey.

    Even the river stones
    show early autumn: wet scarlet,
    sugar-maple bronze.

PASCHAL LETTER

A Flemish wife?
          Flanders
I suppose.
          I used to stop
for every hawk dead along the road,
pull the tails for Emerson,
his beaded prayer fans.

Regards from
at the wheel, coming in
from airy points outland.

Of Irish memories, the ones
that hang most fondly:
country men beside country lanes,
that quick sideways jerk
of the head, twitch of the lips
in formal greeting, as if
to signal, "Boy, it's
a tough one" or "Aye,
it's a life alright."

This little-traveled highway
made me think of that, I guess.
That and the men in cafés

these last four days
speaking softly of elementals
like rain and wind and hay.

I cut north to Beecher Island
about noon
for an Easter stretch, dropped down
off the plains into the crease
of the Arikaree—
a good honest place
for it, out of sight
of the Horizon King, out of the wind:
a quiet bridge, an open grove
with a paschal breeze.
Of course the Cheyenne battle
there, the death of Roman Nose,
lends a dialectical glamour,
even a hint of "noble rot."
But mostly airy amplitude
and sweet-tooth thoughts.
I pictured your garden
there—May your radishes be up—

and the words of Finn:
"Spring is the strong time /
The heath spreads out
its long hair / Its face
is beautiful / The cuckoos
singing and ever singing . . ."

Those are my people.

And what if the clue
in the "Saltwater case"
is the Down Eastern term she used
for the lull between breaking
waves: *slatch?*

       Six deer,
creased brows, looking back—
they miss the tulip trees!?!

This time of day some days
I miss the tulip trees.
Let's leave it at that.

CRADLE KNOLL

All the bloodhounds in the world
touch down. Wardens come from miles around.

Last night a lazy dream, footage of a full range
tossing under storm, wild zydeco wind
up from the south via Hurricane Gap, leaves
in the air, gullies surging, foaming brick-red—
Van Gogh's hair, sickle-cut, or General Sherman's.

Grouse drum on hazy ridges.
Down the road a place called Muses Mills.
White-throated sparrows sing their whispersong.

> *All the bloodhounds*
> *in the world*
> can't pin it down.

from **THE ROAD TO TOWN**

Cars driving all day over acorns
and pignuts fallen on the road, crackling
and popping—the children laughing all day
at the endless hours of it.

Sidings, seats of the moon.

Found in a glove box:

The waves ran to meet us,
even the ocean loved your skin.
Redstart woman.

The retriever dove for snapper,
brought them in and dropped them
at our feet. Ceviche, soon.

"The waves ran to meet them"—
Jays still talk about it
summer afternoons.

SKY IN AMBER

Playful thunder's
rumbling freight-train vowels
soft and low, on and on
like a proud Lao name.

Cordial apparitions
come and go on the lawn:
a man in a porkpie, slim, a bit tattered,
as if looking for food. Hawk, dear friend,
smiling, holding up a handsome bass.

The skin of our teeth.

I'd like to see
Sovranes Creek, walk it whistling down
till it loses its own sweet
time of mind in the sea.

SEMPER FI

On my birthday
Ocracoke

Wet sand holds the transcript,
dry sand lets it blow—

sanderling codex filigree
hurries through the lulls. Thirty knots,

red knots tide, retied:
tiny x's crossing tiny y's.

A laughing girl sets mouse traps
for the gulls.

MIDNIGHT COFFEE

Rigel shines
on occupied territories,
occupied times—

the *diction* of the stars.

KNOCK ON

"Wet sidewalks"—nods to the dead.
The first tomatoes carved and set
sashimi-style. Someone had a shrunken head.
Someone's family had a souvenir shrunken head
they brought out now and then for parties,
or dinner guests on Sunday afternoons.
And all the animals got up
and quietly left the room.

A *NOSTOS* FOR
JOHNNY NEVER MISSES

Still here, still there,
that promissory place on Cheyenne River
where we stopped a dozen times
to see the waters, watch the hills,
sat without a word.

Stopped to take the waters
when their colors rise and the hills
fathom and fade, still there,
gently covered for the night
like a canary's cage.

ELEGY 1024

The first off-guard days of September,
tether cut, float like gulls
over jetsam. Cicada with jays—
Whispersong of the radiant shanghaied.
I want to see you ten more times.

AKER INKLING

A cuckoo slips
through the young May day—
bright eyes, wet lips.

SALAL

1.

Dark waters
at the foot of the mountain:
Salal: Salal muckamuck

(to wet a finger
in the pidgin wind).
We sleep arm in arm

beneath clement Pendletons,
wake to find pines
between people on the south

lagoon. The Great Dane wrote the Sea
is simply often
the first to say *No*—stars

soon to follow. Breakers
exPLODE, the running
of the gulls, aiheee.

2.

Shag. Shell.
"Boy Cleaning Fish."
Geishas once whitened
their faces with powdered
droppings of the nightingale.
But then beyond, half a mile
out, through the glasses we pick up
scoters, there beyond the surf
and surge, hundreds in an open
flock, the main corps, true scoter,
riding swells, all facing
north: cordon and cortex
of the kind, in speciality:
and that they tear off
mussels to swallow them whole
and the gizzards grind them
Beowúlfian
to the brilliant obsidian/
purple sand we find in
wandering driftlines on the beach—
called *scoter dust* or
scoter meal, aiheee.

3 .

I heard your horse
this morning
calling Opus 17.

Muddy boys gut
hapless ling.
Heartwood

in sumptuary stanzas
far-to-sea. At dawn
the first headlights

around the 101 bend,
northbound, sweep
the mysteries: clean

hills close together,
cowrie smile. Thin
red ink squeezed

from blue salal.
And poetry will surely
win—what could stand up

to such a force
pounding the shores
nightlong day

after day? aiheee.

Apple wine
        high in the mountains:
Hollyhocks still bloom
        with autumn all around them:
Fourth of July girls
        pigeon-toed
in a gold September room.

SWANNANOA

Who called that little orchid "Three Birds,"
the Simpler's Joy was on her.

Simpler's Joy,
as in Dowland's Galliard
or Purcell's Pavan.

The mountains missing leaves,
low sun: pearled, pebbled, bossed—
hints of plum, glints of elderberry, almost
a calico.

Kinglets tumble to green river cane,
curious about this crooked little path
fishermen use to get down along the stream.

EVEN NEAR SALTWATER

Even near saltwater
remembering with What's-her-name's daughter
how the Tsistsistas when they lived

long ago near the Rees on the upper Missouri
were so taken by the local beans—
their glamorous uniform blond-beige—

that when they later moved west
out onto the high plains and first saw
the endless prairie-dog towns

and the hundreds of identical creatures
scurrying toward their dens
the women laughed and thought

of a cascade of those pretty beans
tumbling into a kettle
and called the animals by the same

name, *ononi wonski,*
"Ree beans," and the meanings embraced,
intertwined

and went on to walk and talk
and ride and someday die together
ever since those times.

FOR JIM

What a wonderful place for a hat to blow off—
bouncing and tumbling away half a mile
down Boxelder Creek and into the big river breaks.

THE OAKS HAVE YET TO BREAK

Burgundy in autumn
reminded me first glance
of the upper South, Kentucky, and now
the favor bounces back, here, not only
because of the wine-red vines in the trees.
Fishing again in the fall
of an election year, the new tilt to the botany
like the odd tilt on a globe
in an antiquarian's window, and the hills
packed with delicacies arm's length
for the taking. The mass of walnuts alone
along this valley could sink a *Bismarck*.
Fake woolly worm, fake katydid.
Late in the Second War the Hellions
were even scheming to bomb schools of fish.
Black oak leaves wind down to mustard yellow.
Kingfisher dives, flies up empty, shaking head.
Maybe a few crumbs of Bleu de Bresse
will make the river come alive.

BLUE RIDGE: BLOSSOMS ON THE FERAL TREES

Apple blossoms on the feral trees
have a light all their own, cool ivory
of petals already fallen. One mile,

maybe two, north from Beetree,
a hint of wind nudged through the gap,
the slightest sleight-of-hand. Two miles,

maybe three—*stung* ivory, coinage
of stars—new leaves on the beech sprouts
silken enough to swaddle a child.

HIGH IN THE BIGHORNS

Indian grass in August
the colors of wild plum
and honey.

Streams drop away.
The swirling earth.
The rivers as reins.

from **FALL (THE SEASONS)**

Winds of El Niño
made the earth spin faster,
days shorter
by three-thousandths
of a second. Guard dogs whined
around the Museum of Time,
Rockford, Illinois.

We climbed the hill
(a mountain-hill, Big Sur)
with bedrolls and a bag
of avocados and slept
up there one night.

In fact
we moved across the continent
east to west
in the classical manner
and came to California
and found the avocados cheap,
bought fifteen or twenty

and proceeded straight
to the coast (knelt
to the bull kelp) and directly

up the hill. It seemed
the obvious thing to do—

early fall, a glint
in the chapparal, and made
a camp at the very top,
sat crosslegged for enormous sunset,
black gorge of Pacific night . . .

Every now and then an avocado.
Twinkle of distant trawler lights.
The mind rode in the heart.

   To seek that which was lost
without knowing seeking
or that it was ever gone.

   To make a certain noise
with the lips, as in calling
a dog.

   Avocado,
plucked from Nahuatl ahuacatl:
"testicle."   ·

Atlatl touché.
Pardon the French,
'tis a showery day.

    And these are Bach's
bones. A photo from the Bach-Archiv
in Leipzig, 1895, framed
above the telephone.
                        Spinal chord
massive, broad shoulders, thin thighs,
ample ribcage, dark
through the eyes. A measuring tape
runs up one side.
Most of the right-hand fingers
gone, vaporized perhaps from all that
fluttering in the high parts.
The skull seems small
in relation.
                    But then
it's fall—
                The mind moves
into the heart.

Three Diaries

ORIOLE DIARY

Friday: The last time here it was August. We camped among the public lilac bushes and promised to return one spring to see them in bloom.

Now, in latter May, we sit among them—six parallel rows one hundred yards long: lavenders and ivories and purples ten feet tall.

We sit in scented public air and talk about the streamsides thick with wild currant blossom, the sweet yellow blow of the sweet black currants, and vow to come back one fall for the plucking.

Saturday: Bloomtime: continuous though staggered aspect of the world: whitecapping to water, poetry amid the general tongue.

Orioles dominate this oasis grove of elms and cottonwoods buffering the lilac plantation from Dakota winds. Their calls and dartings fill the air like the lilacs.

Three hundred years ago this spring, Basho departed on his trajectory through the Far North in search of poetic compounds. Everything within the present 48-hour Sensorium—the billowing trees, the lay of the far hills, this fire of lilac twigs—what they have of English on them is, by poetic tide and instigation, for him.

Sunday: Midday, just after church, a steady trickle of visitors from town, twelve miles north, drive slowly through the grove to see the lilacs: elderly couples, groups of white-haired ladies in floral dresses. Occasionally a car stops on the far side to snitch a mixed bouquet: *Lilac Thieves:* a painting (say, Sargent), a daguerreotype, a quick French film.

We sit idling in calm sun and whistle cheap imitations of oriole songs just good enough to bring the males in, bristling and flashing, swooping in overhead to check the stranger with the terrible voice. After two days of their constant comings and goings through the trees, their oranges sizzling, there is a sense of them lacing the air, stitching it with their continuous vectors, wrapping the grove, webbing and fastening the place. (The birds and myself and the Ornithology Club of Osaka see it this way.)

Hot dogs on lilac hot dog sticks: Downwind from smoke and splash and blossom.

Forks of Grand River
South Dakota, 1989

TREEHOUSE *HAIBUN*

for Robert Harris

Dear Robert. I'm sitting here with a cold cup of coffee and a cigarette, thinking half-thoughts over a dozen treehouse photographs spread across the table—shots taken during the past three weeks (in a bit of a hurry: the leaves are coming on fast), ever since it hit me. They no doubt deserve better—a wide-angle Canaletto treatment maybe, with a lazy Flies and Grounders in the distance or a fisherman kneeling by a stream. But the fuzzy Instamatic isn't all wrong when it comes to information easily mistaken for a dream.

A month ago in Lawrence, Kansas, I was walking off a night at Bryant's Barbecue, ambling along in the woods between the Santa Fe tracks and the River Kaw. Paused beside a rancid brook, I spotted a wonderful treehouse in a big cottonwood across the way. It must have been sixty feet up without a branch between it and the ground. At the time, anyway, it seemed an engineering masterpiece: the logistics of hauling the lumber up there; even planting the ladder boards along the way. I had passed the shambles of a plywood hut earlier and dismissed it after a brief inspection as an ordinary clubhouse—but this thing was more mysterious. I couldn't imagine anyone's father building one quite that high in such an uncompromising tree. Two possibilities hung in the March air: a very inspired high-school shop class, or a team of enlightened and well-organized hobos who knew just what they wanted—Peace and Altitude.

From that morning on I began seeing them everywhere: while driving around the countryside, walking through small towns, from train windows. Back home in Ohio I even began remembering specimens I didn't know I'd seen, would hop in the car and drive out with the camera. Most of the time, there it was, if nothing more than a board or two. I was thrown hostile looks, treated like a celebrity, and chased by dogs.

In a few days I was mildly obsessed with their frequency and their wilting silhouettes in the bare trees like (very much like) Chinese characters crumbling above the tracks. Ruins, that's the word—sweeter than wasted abbey. Castaway, water-soluble ruins, monuments to that semi-private childhood *mondo obligato* composed of near-forgotten close-ups of mud between house and shrubbery, or random lint and hair-pin landscapes on the rug behind the sofa.

But at this time of year, the season of their highest profile, they enter the public domain to loom in a marginal Commons: the one-man band suddenly joined at an intersection by the medieval percussion instrument that sounds like the clapping-along of several hands. And for these weeks, the quietly insistent visions of their presence, out there in the dusk, town after town, drift in each night full of orphan Peace and Altitude, until the April leaves fill out, take over till October . . .

*

That one atilt in a Norway maple, Satin Street, with sundown robins scolding.

Down the block, one in a sprawling elm, three bikes leaning on their kickstands below, and boys trading: a scrap of deer hide for an eye cup and a brass prong.

One in a linden.

One in an ash, with heat lightning.

One with a mattress.

One with a bathroom.

One with a hookah.

One demolished for firewood.

One in a pear. *Pears for Sale*.

One lost in Hurricane Hazel.

One with a spiral staircase, cool in the summer, warm in the winter.

One out of the blue at a swank soiree: along an entire wall of the living room, a row of craggy bonsais in tiny rock gardens. Halfway up in a fifteen-incher near the window perched a treehouse, in perfect scale, nice but not too fancy, made of split and broken tongue depressors.

One with a crow's nest.

Quiet neighborhood, happy apple.

One in a master willow.

One with a fireman's pole.

Early American in the mountains: "No whites, blacks or Indians."

One with pea shooters.

A colony in a beech grove.

One in a dead sycamore behind a shopping center. We walked
back through muck and weeds. "I was born up there."

One demolished for dog house.

One with a spitoon.

One in a redwood.

One with a snoring man on the lam.

One with a maid.

One with fishing poles.

One half-full of snow.

One with a canary.

One with a dictionary.

One with portholes, overlooking the sea.

1980

WARBLER *HAIBUN*

Knocker—not his real name—asks me why I write about my hometown all the time. I usually refer him to Mississippi John Hurt's "Avalon's my hometown / It's always on my mind." And the old Asian haiku men who knew where they came from and what's the weather there. And the Aranda people of Australia: Their entire lives they mention their native places with respectful tears in their eyes.

You can recognize a person with a hometown in her heart. She moves a little differently, speaks a bit more slowly and particularly. Her words have solid forms behind them; they hang from an actual trellis.

I am standing at the solid place where little Sam's Creek joins the larger Whetstone Creek. All around are lovely slender sycamores, young buckeye trees and box elders, wild ginger, bluebells and ramps. Beyond the confluence, lean teenage tulip trees climb high into the air. I've known this intersection half a century. I know its roots and its branches. Between the singing birds I hear dogs bark from beyond the river.

An old half-dead
vaguely familiar cherry stump,
hide like a black rhino.

Even in that small village
we bought berets in high school,
two or three of us.

A house wren hops about the honeysuckle, singing. I remember
the one who sang during my mother's graveside rites, and then
more distant specimens as mentioned down through the barber-
shop-mirrored years—John Clare, William Blake, Saigyo—and I
think of Poetic Precedent, pervasive precedent, as in Law, Com-
mon Law: a sense of shared commonality and transgenerational
connection, a durable poetic connection, not repeated or aped,
but simply absorbed. Although poetry tends to gravitate toward
those points and issues where even legal precedent admits, "the
Constitution is *absolutely silent.*"

This catbird
obviously studied with
the great grosbeak, Pheucticus.

A wet wren.
The ghost of Mr. Goosey Kidwell—
Native soil.

The first two days of my visit were cool and rainy.

In under a beech tree
out of the rain—
listening to the wood thrush.

Through the wet woods—
from wood thrush
to wood thrush.

In the dark rain
the black-throated blue could be
a blue-throated black.

The following days were clear and bright, all the doors were open.
I circled the twin lakes slowly each morning, sometimes twice.

Across the young
maple leaves—shadow
of a wood thrush.

One black-throated green
drifting north—
the world gets better.

The parula high
high up, passes for
a bumble bee.

Magnolia warbler
in full sun—we meet
again and again.

Nashville warbler
lost deep in a box elder—
the master plan.

A string of haiku—
a string of pack mules—
bearing small breakable birds.

Under this very tree
thirty years ago—
interrupted by a wood thrush.

I hate to leave
that wood thrush
all alone.

Snake birds
mating wildly
in the sunny treetops.

The blue-wing
looks tired. Let's rechristen it
the Shawnee warbler.

Sycamore warbler—
life of lives, high in
the moon-colored branches.

Canada warbler
up for air—fine black streaks
on the throat of a yellow iris.

The chestnut-sided—
all the colors of a girlchild
in a garden.

At last, the bay-breast
drops down. Aye, to be
watched by such a bird!

May 2006

p. 30, *doll's eyes*: white baneberry, a plant of the eastern woodlands.

p. 139, *Vogelsang*: aka Roger Birdsong, a friend from early Ohio school days.

p. 176, *Finn*: early Irish culture hero and primal poet.

p. 180, *Sovranes Creek*: a stream mentioned in Robinson Jeffers' poem "The Place for No Story" as "the noblest place I have ever seen."

p. 184, *Nostos*: (newly minted) poetic genre: a conjuring of a cherished place or landscape from one's past. From the Greek "nostos," return home. A root of "nostalgia."

p. 187, *salal*: an abundant, blue-berried shrub of the Oregon coast. The "great Dane" is, of course, Isak Dinesen.

p. 193, *Tsistsistas*: the Cheyenne people's name for themselves as a tribe.

Poems in this selection previously appeared in the following books and chapbooks:

Light Years (Blue Wind Press, 1977), poem on p. 9
River through Rivertown (The Figures, 1982), poems on pp. 1 and 20
Satin Street (Moyer Bell, 1997), poems beginning on pp. 2, 3, 7, 10, 12, 17, 18, 21, 22, 29, 31, 32, 38, 57
The Seasons (Adventures in Poetry, 2002), poems beginning on pp. 11, 49, 139, 141, 142, 149, 167, 198
Small Weathers (Qua Books, 2004), poems beginning on pp. 8, 45, 64, 66, 69, 70, 74, 81, 110, 111, 147, 166, 185

Undanceable (Flood Editions, 2005), poems beginning on pp. 55, 59, 91, 187

The Bark of the Dog (Flood Editions, 2010), poems beginning on pp. 30, 39, 54, 62, 82, 85, 86, 98, 156, 164, 175

Treehouse Haibun (Longhouse, 2010), beginning on p. 205

Warbler Haibun (Longhouse, 2011), beginning on p. 211

Harpsichord Hills (Horse Less Press, 2013), poems beginning on pp. 42, 44, 63, 100

Red Mavis (Flood Editions, 2014), poems beginning on pp. 43, 47, 48, 53, 60, 73, 80, 88, 104, 107, 108, 109, 155, 161, 174, 178, 182, 186, 191, 192, 196, 197

Would-be Dogwood (Shirt Pocket Press, 2016), poems beginning on pp. 56, 65, 84, 87, 90, 99, 103, 173, 180, 181, 194, 195

Stars Seen Then (Partly Press, 2020), poems beginning on pp. 61, 79, 162, 179, 183, 184, 193

The Panicle (Butternut Books, 2021), poems beginning on pp. 101, 151

Tunes Meant for Whistling (Longhouse, 2021), poems beginning on p. 127